Under The Magnolia Trees

My Childhood Memories

Rebecca Morgan

chipmunkapublishing
the mental health publisher

Rebecca Morgan

Published by
Chipmunkapublishing
PO Box 6872
Brentwood
Essex CM13 1ZT
United Kingdom

http://www.chipmunkapublishing.com

Copyright © Rebecca Morgan 2010

Edited by Aleks Lech

Chipmunkapublishing gratefully acknowledge the support of Arts Council England.

ARTS COUNCIL ENGLAND

Author Biography

Rebecca Morgan was born in Hertfordshire in 1951. She obtained a degree in Modern History and Politics from Sheffield University in 1973, followed by a Post-Graduate Diploma in Librarianship from Birmingham Polytechnic in 1975.

In 1978 she became a Chartered Librarian and recently retired after 20 years with Sheffield Libraries, Archives and Information Service.

She has experienced severe depression, postnatal depression and psychotic illness during her life.

Rebecca is married with one son and lives in Sheffield. This is her second book, following her vivid picture of her years of mental illness in Hertfordshire and Sheffield portrayed in her first book: "The Nest of Sanity" also published by Chipmunka Publishing.

Rebecca Morgan is a pseudonym.

Author of 'The Nest of Sanity' 2008

Cover photograph of Osborne road taken by the author.

Rebecca Morgan

"One writes only for oneself and if what one writes enriches other people's lives in any way, that is a side-effect bonus."

Bernice Rubens

Rebecca Morgan

Dedication

This book is dedicated to my three brothers and my sister, hoping that they recognise the picture I have painted for them. I thank them with love for being there for me.

Rebecca Morgan

Acknowledgements

Thanks as always to my loving and supportive husband, to my son and to my family. Thanks also to my good friends for listening to me talk extensively about my writing on many occasions. Lastly, thanks to my late Mum and Dad without whom I would not have had these childhood experiences.

Rebecca Morgan

Author's Note

Some of the names in this book have been changed to protect the privacy of family and friends. I do not intend to cause offence to any person by the writing of this book.

Rebecca Morgan

Under The Magnolia Trees

Walking paths that we walked as children
Hand in hand, or bike followed bike.
Figures of eight past the post box
Or cops and robbers, a game that we liked.

Watching ripples and waves on the river
Throwing pebbles in the self same stream
Searching the long grass for bottles
Discarded where picnickers had been.

Snatching our pleasures like apples
From neighbours' high branches we stole
And snuggled them up to our pillows
For feasts after midnight had tolled.

Sometimes we'd dress from the tin chest
Old garments and coats – what a sight!
Small plays we would act with bravado
Of kings, young princesses and knights.

Swinging from our garage rafters
Over the gravelly drive
Out over the treetops and house roofs
Up to the sky I would dive.

We searched for green moss for dish gardens
For stones and elastic bands
For lollipop sticks and old pennies
At the kerb, under hedgerows we scanned.

Together we'd pool all our findings
Not much, but in those days a store
Little things; but somehow those friendships
We'd treasure forever - and more …

Rebecca Morgan

Under The Magnolia Trees

The Garden

My favourite trees in our garden were the two magnolia trees at the front of the house. The story went that they were brought over from China as seedlings years ago. When flowering they were absolutely beautiful to me, and my bedroom (shared with my sister) had a large bay window overlooking the branches. These flowers would eventually drop, leaving a carpet made of pink and creamy white petals. These trees still stand today and when I look up into their branches a whole raft of memories from my childhood bursts into my mind.

****

The untamed privet hedge opened out to a gateless drive. There must have been a gate once, for the old green gate posts still stood. The drive swept upwards past a red-berried holly tree to a battered neglected garage once painted green; the paint long since chipped and weathered away. The large brick house, fronted by two bay windows, wasn't much noticed by me – I hurried past, to the garden.

Once it may have been an elegant place with rows of shrubs, twenty trees of russet apples in an orchard to the left, fruit bushes and a small wood of fir trees at the far distance. Once cared for, now neglected, this garden was splendid to me. Strawberries, raspberries, blackberries, redcurrants – all were tasted in their season. Pears and apples were scrumped and hoarded for a midnight feast. Fir cones, conkers and acorns were eagerly collected. Soft lush green moss was gently prised with a blunt knife from a broken brick wall and used to create small dish gardens.

With a broken bit of mirror (from a forgotten handbag) as a pond, a fir cone as a tree, and small stones as a path, my miniature world would hold enchantment.

Flowers, once tended, now sprang up carelessly amongst the long grass, bindweed and bracken. Daffodils still bloomed in season, forget-me-nots and snapdragons and of course the buttercups, celandines and dandelions. We would play tag amongst the trees, or climb up into their branches. Once we even strung up an old wicker chair to an overhanging branch of a large tree and made a rustic swing. Another time I fell from a tree into a patch of stinging nettles and was sore from stings on my legs and arms. Towards the far end of the garden was a small green gate; we would sit astride this and swing back and forth in accord with the squeaking hinges. The soil here was wet with clay, and once there had been a shed, for the concrete foundations still remained. We would make our camp here; this was our centre, our meeting place; nobody from outside our gang was allowed to trespass here. Kids from the surrounding houses and from the nearby St. Catherine's Road often played with us in the garden and we were a ragamuffin lot, rather scruffy (sometimes we'd be in our vests and navy knickers!) so that one or two neighbours in particular complained at the state of us and the garden. Dad never took any notice of the comments.

I often devised my own games of imagination. I had a small bicycle wheel of white rubber tied to a piece of rope which I called my 'Horsey'. I would drag it around making whinnying noises for hours on end. My reading was often stories about gymkhanas and lucky posh girls who owned a horse. In reality I was scared of the real animals as they were so tall and powerful, and I never had riding lessons like my older sister Caroline did. As sisters we used to be rivals for our parents' attention and sometimes used to fight with hair pulling and scratching of faces. Caroline usually won as I was much smaller than her. I was jealous of my sister from an early age because of her confidence, a trait which I lacked. Also she was popular and I struggled to make friends. I used to follow Caroline around a lot in the garden and surrounding roads and she used to try and shake me off, especially if she was meeting her friends, two whole years older than me!

My brother Stuart built a tree house, by name only, as it was just a table top platform balanced between two branches. With my brother Henry, Stuart set fire to the privet hedge at the end of the garden, much to my Dad's annoyance. Once, my eldest two brothers dug a big hole down at the bottom of the garden and held me and my sister captive in a clay dungeon, covered by an old table top. Frightened by spiders and nameless creepy crawlies, we screamed till rescued. I have had a fear of spiders ever since. On one occasion when quite small I ran down the garden and jumped, only to land with one foot in an ants' nest. Transfixed with panic, I watched in horror as the myriad creatures darted up my bare leg; then my yells brought help and my brother Stuart swung me high in his arms, brushing off the offending midgets. One frightening day, a herd of cows which had escaped from a nearby farm trespassed up the drive and I ran in fear to tell Mum, who was as usual at work in the kitchen. We huddled together in the sitting room having bolted the door and shut the windows. We were both very scared!! Another time, an injured swan from the river appeared on the drive and we had to ring the RSPCA to get it collected

The garden was to us a green land of escape where we played cowboys and Indians and performed amateurish plays; tales of kings and princes, of witches and pitiful babes; written and directed always by my sister Caroline. Our old tin chest contained a mysterious collection of old coats and skirts, scarves and shoes, which added colour to the productions.

When I was first at school I continued to like dressing up and we had old clothes in a box which we could sometimes play with. I was about five or six when I saw for the first time a cheap ruby ring in the bottom of the dressing up box. I coveted this ring and felt that it should by rights be mine, as I didn't have anything like it to be my precious thing. To my chagrin I remember I 'borrowed' this ring and took it home to keep as mine. However when I got home with it, I felt ashamed and guilty and slipped the ring through a crack in the floorboards, where it was never found again. I felt some small satisfaction that no-one at school would get the pleasure of wearing it ever again and only I knew where it lay. When the teacher asked if anyone had seen the ring I said nothing. Years later I wrote a poem about it:

Guilt

It was shiny and red
Big enough, small enough to fit my middle finger
I wore it
When I could
Once a week when Miss Cox said
We could play
Dressing-up.

There were silken clothes
Green pyjamas, a flowered skirt
But it was the ring
I desired.

One time
I took it home
Red, shiny and <u>mine.</u>
I couldn't show, I couldn't tell.
But it was <u>mine.</u>

When Miss Cox asked
Who has seen the ring?
Who has lost the ring?
I was silent.

Under the floor
Through a crack
I dropped it carefully.
I never told,
Till now.

Writers Class, Sheffield October 1994.

When sold to developers by my dad, our garden became a building site and my older brothers played battles in the muddy workmen's trenches, spinning old 78 records in a noisy war of brittle crashing missiles. Three detached houses were built on the land, our childhood haven was splintered and our fun dispersed. Those thrills and games were almost lost forever, but they still linger on in our adult minds and dreams.

The House and Family

The house and garden in Osborne Road, Broxbourne, in Hertfordshire, were to be my home for 17 years. I was born in 1951 in a prefab a mile or so away at Dobbs Weir. The family moved to the big house when I was about 18 months old. We were a motley crew, my Mum and Dad and their five children born over about 10 years. My Dad, Joseph, was Welsh, short in height with originally ginger hair. My Mum, May, was a village lass from Debden in Essex and was not worldly wise; indeed she struggled to keep pace with our hectic lives. I have two elder brothers, Henry and Stuart, and one younger, Graham. My sister Caroline is two years older than me. Together with cats, a dog and various other pets (hedgehog, guinea pig and rabbit) we tumbled around the ground floor of the house and the garden, filling the air with shouts, screams and cries.

My eldest brother, Henry, was slim with brown hair. He was good natured, honest and kind, with a strong sense of right and wrong. He was always reliable and in later years became the head of the family, taking the main role in caring for my parents. When I had periods of mental health problems he was always there for me and supported my parents throughout. Henry left the Secondary Modern School (at Broxbourne) and trained to be a hairdresser; he was always on hand to give the family free haircuts, taking over from Dad who could only do men's hairstyles (or 'pudding basin' cuts, which we hated.) He liked music and playing records on his prize possession of a Dansette record player, and after a spell of cycling grew fond of tinkering with his second-hand 'bangers'. He loved the river, had two boats and worked for a while on the market gardens along the river near Nazeing.

Stuart, who dallied with motorbike riding for a while, soon followed his brother's example and worked on our drive, customising his latest car. (Car parts on the cooker top and in the small kitchen were nothing out of the ordinary.) He also put together a Lotus 7 sports car from a kit. Stuart had brown hair which he teased into a quiff with his comb and (like me) had the slight plump figure of a typical Welsh descendent. He went to the Hertford Boys Grammar School. My fellow pupils at the girls' Grammar School always teased me about my handsome brother. He was sometimes a bit pensive and quiet and he didn't always see eye to eye with our Dad. He was out a lot with his friends and we didn't see him much in the house. Both boys acquired girlfriends pretty soon, Henry's school friend later became his fiancée and wife of over forty years! Stuart also worked at the market gardens and then had jobs at a bank, Addis in Hertford and selling Ever Ready products in London. Eventually he followed his dream to travel the world with a friend, expanding his talent for languages. I always got on well with Stuart and missed him when he was away.

My youngest brother, Graham, was slim and good looking. He was a gentle character and quite shy. He also went to the Secondary Modern School and pretty much hated it. He grew his hair very long in the 70's and sported a wooden cross around his neck. He liked science fiction novels and enjoyed music by John Mayall, classical guitarist John Williams and the Beatles. He helped my Mum with the garden and later on trained in horticulture and has since enjoyed a good career in gardening. I spent a lot of my childhood hours playing with Graham, exploring the local area. He also writes, mostly poems, which describe the nature all around him, which he loves. At the age of twenty he became a Christian and is still active in his local church.

Caroline was taller than me, slightly plump and had shoulder length brown hair, which was always shiny. This was courtesy of Sunsilk shampoo which in those days we bought in small sachets. She seemed to be always hungry and used to eat up all the leftovers on the others' plates at meal times! Caroline is two years older than me and I was always rather jealous of her. She did well at school and excelled in English and drama, which was illustrated by her performances in the school plays. She and I used to bicker a lot. She was naturally cheerful and confident whereas I was often down in the dumps. (Graham called me 'Moaning Minnie'.) Caroline was mostly sociable, a characteristic which only came to me when I was older. I stayed at home and studied long term while she managed to complete her school work more quickly and was able to meet her friends and do activities such as riding lessons. We were quite different as children, but later in life became good friends. I had joined Brownies but didn't stay long. Caroline persevered and became a Girl Guide and later was appointed Head Girl at the Grammar School. She was always a warm, caring sister and very helpful to my mother. She left home at eighteen to train as a teacher.

I was a skinny short girl with tangled hair which I didn't bother to comb. My mum used to try and catch me to sit me down so she could brush my unruly curls before school. I only started putting on weight from about age fifteen. I was a quiet studious child, spending hours on homework and reading. I was moody and continually anxious. I used to enjoy the music of The Beatles, Elvis, and Simon and Garfunkel, which I played when possible in the living room. I grew to love the songs of Nana Mouskouri which now evoke memories of a chapter of my childhood in the house at Osborne Road.

The house then, in the 1950's and 60's was much more down at heel than it is today. It badly needed roof repairs but we never found the money to get it done. It needed pointing and painting but we didn't bother much with those sorts of things. Inside, the wallpaper was peeling off though Mum did make an effort to decorate occasionally, in addition to all her other work. The toilet was outside and this was a great embarrassment to me when my school friends came for tea. The sitting room which also served as a dining room was known to the family as 'the other room'. Quite why, I'm not sure. There were two large bay windows with wide window seats which I loved to sit on, always with a book in hand, gazing out and day dreaming. These seats were once painted orange to match the wallpaper but ended their lives as green which was more pleasing to the eye. We had a square of thin dark green carpet in the centre of the room surrounded by oddments of lino, and my Dad's favourite red armchair was under the front window. Here he sat smoking Senior Service cigarettes (or his pipe which I liked the smell of), and drinking Guinness. He would watch the news programmes obsessively (as I do now) or the snooker programme 'Pot Black', which was hard to follow in black and white! He enjoyed tea and used to make it by boiling the water inside the aluminium teapot directly on the gas hob! He used about 12 teaspoons of tea and we used to say you could stand the spoon up in it! Another favourite of his was listening to 'Letter from America' by Alistair Cooke on the radio each morning. Dad had the unusual habit of buttering the bread on the loaf before slicing it; he assured me this was the Welsh way!

Under The Magnolia Trees

My parents had the main bedroom, which had been divided to create another small bedroom with one single bed and two bunks. Here during our early years I slept and played in this limited space with Caroline and Graham. My sister had the upper bunk due to her seniority; my hair used to get caught in its wire springs when I sat up in the lower bunk. Some years later a new staircase was put in so the two girls could sleep with privacy in one of the upstairs bedrooms. This bedroom had a locked door which connected through to the three flats let by my Dad. I often had nightmares about the tenants sneaking into our bedroom at night through this door to harm us. Out of the bay window of this room was the lovely view of the flowering magnolia trees in the early summer. I lived here with my sister Caroline who left a trail of clothes from the door to her bed every night, and then dressed in reverse route the next day. I had my ornaments and my writing paper (I loved writing and receiving letters) stored in the lovely walnut dressing table with its tiny drawers and a triptych of mirrors. Caroline was mad on Elvis Presley and I copied her and joined his fan club, though secretly liking Cliff better. We had a phase of going to the cinema to see the Cliff and Elvis spectaculars, and Caroline had their posters on the walls and scratched the name of her idol on the white painted window ledge with a pin.

My older brothers shared a bedroom near the kitchen and the cellar door. Stuart was away a lot once he found his travel legs so Henry used that room mostly. In it were a series of servant bells from the old days when Osborne Road was a wealthy street. Henry was the first to get a small record player, and played his records by Duane Eddy, Bill Haley, Buddy Holly, Eddie Cochrane and the like. Stuart had some French music by Charles Aznavour which I loved to listen to. My sister and I had a reel to reel tape recorder which we squabbled about, but had much fun with. We were able to record songs from the radio. My Mum's favourite tunes were 'Scarlet Ribbons' by Harry Belafonte and 'Please Don't Go' by Donald Peers. She also liked the piano concertos by Tchaikovsky and Rachmaninov. Some nights after playing music in their room either or both of my elder brothers would escape via their bedroom window (on the ground floor) and return the same way after an evening of exploits. When Dad found out he was furious!

The cellar was dark and damp and water rats came into it from the brook across the road. We kept coal down there and odd bits of old furniture like tables which we did not need any more. I was frightened to go down there at all, but one day I was shocked when I leant casually against the cellar door and fell backwards down the stone steps, bruising myself. That door was always kept locked, but that day someone had forgotten to do it. The passage which ran from the 'other room' to the original front door housed the coats and mackintoshes of different sizes and hues for the whole family. To separate the front door from our motley crew and to keep it private for the tenants, Dad put up a piece of hardboard which could be opened and closed by sliding it to one side. I loved going through this 'door' to collect the post which arrived on the mat in the hall. I always scampered quickly though, as a tenant would sometimes appear and I was in awe of them. I still dream of that partition to this day, and the thrill of finding a letter from a friend on the mat.

It was a large house and my Dad let half of it as three flats. He wasn't a very caring landlord and was forever having arguments with the tenants, complaining when the rent was late or when there was loud music played. On the other hand, certain tenants got their own back, when moving out, by deliberately leaving the gas taps on or by encouraging mice or rats by leaving scraps of food on the floor of the little kitchen. (In fact for several months one year I heard the scratching noises of a mouse under our bedroom floorboards until my Dad disposed of the creature). My Mum and I always had the job of cleaning the flats after tenants left. Dad advised me never to be a landlord when I grew up. He must have made some money when he sold most of the garden to a developer, but we never saw much of it. Three detached modern houses were built in the sixties and we were left with an oblong patch of lawn at the back of the house where Graham grew vegetables. Dad made a small putting green and taught Graham to walk up and down on an old beer barrel. Once, on a trip to the country, he saw an old tin snail sit-on toy and brought it home for us to play with. It was brightly coloured and remained in the garden for years. In the green wooden garage at the side of the house Dad rigged up a swing from the rafters made of strong rope, and I loved whiling away the hours on that swing. When you went upwards there was a lovely view down the gravel drive to the road and the brook and field across the road. As soon as I got older a small housing estate called Hallmores was built on that field.

Rebecca Morgan

Making Ends Meet

We were always poor and Mum struggled to make ends meet. My Dad dolled out the cash very begrudgingly and Mum, in those days, never had any money to spend on herself. She had an old white china cup, lacking a handle, in which she kept her loose change and the housekeeping money. It was common for us to borrow from 'the cup' (as we called it) and to owe to the cup when we needed school dinner money or another small expense; invariably there was not enough to cover our needs. Dad never got used to the new currency which came with decimalisation in 1971, and always continued to talk in 'old money'.

The local corner shop, Reg's, had a system where you had a small red coloured cashbook where your purchases were noted down and you were allowed to wait a few weeks before settling up. A sort of 'tick' system of which we took advantage. The shop sold all kinds of things including basic groceries, emergency needs such as plasters and aspirins, shampoo and even hot water bottles. These, I remember, hung on the back of the shop door in a variety of colours. The owners (Reg and his wife) knew our family very well as we were always in there. Mum would say, "Can someone go round to Reg's and fetch a couple of potatoes or we won't have enough chips for tea?" I remember some provisions we bought which you cannot get now, like bottles of Camp coffee (my first introduction to coffee!) and a box of small packets of ingredients to make lemon iced buns. The latter were only made on special occasions such as birthdays or when Henry got engaged. The best times were when we as children were allowed to buy sweets with our meagre pocket money, or money we had earned by bringing lemonade bottles back (you got three old pence for each bottle returned to the shop from which it was bought). The selection was always the same: sweets such as blackjacks (four a penny), sherbet dabs, and small packs of Parma violets, sweet tobacco and lemonade powder. (My Mum preferred mint imperials or Silvermints from Woolworths; she would use these to bribe us to go to bed!) Later these were joined by small bars of Cadbury's chocolate, bars of Five Boys chocolate creams and, joy of joys, raspberry or orange jubblees (sort of triangular frozen ice lollies). I particularly liked tubes of Smarties or packets of coloured Spangles, but if I ate too many the roof of my mouth got sore.

A walk to the shops, whether it was to Reg's or to Broxbourne parade, was a frequent event and I liked being the one responsible for the small number of purchases which we made on Mum's orders.

On Sunday afternoons we would always have a sweet treat and someone would be nominated to cycle to nearby Broxbourne parade where Saville's shop sold a wider selection of goodies. We would look forward to this treat with impatience. One particular Sunday I cycled in my hand-me-down green-rimmed girls' bicycle with the basket at the front. The route involved two short gravel alleys and after taking the purse containing the cash balanced in the basket I cycled off to Saville's. To my great consternation, when I arrived at the shop I found the purse was gone. I hurriedly retraced my steps, but no sign of the blue purse. It must have bounced out of the basket while I was negotiating the gravel paths. Shamefacedly, I had to return home empty-handed, and my Dad would not pay out for another round of sweets, so I was very unpopular for a day or two.

Our kitchen was small, next to the back door. Mum had a big boiler in which she heated water for the washing of clothes and bed sheets. I think she originally had a wringer too. She later had a small spin dryer which jumped around when in motion. Monday was always wash day and my sister and I had to help with wringing clothes or hanging wet things on the line. We also helped by laying the table, peeling vegetables, washing up and going to Reg's. The boys, however, seemed to avoid the domestic chores and were trained to fetch sticks from the garden or coal from the cellar for the fire. We had an open fire in the 'other room', on which we used to toast bread which was a lovely treat. We had a metal toasting fork for that purpose, which had been made by Henry in school metal work classes. Once, my brother Graham, as a toddler, thought he would help to tidy up by heaping random items on the fire behind the guard, and managed to set fire to the carpet. Luckily the alarm was raised and the fire extinguished. We had no bathroom for many years and were washed in a tin bath in front of the fire. Eventually we had a bathroom of sorts, very narrow and long which my sister painted bright red!

The girls learnt to cook gradually and Dad also liked to have a go. His liver and onions and his stew were marvellous to us, and greedily scoffed. We had a pattern to our days, with certain meals being always eaten on certain days of the week. A firm favourite was egg and chips but we also had beef stew (from the cheapest cuts of stewing steak),liver, fish, corned beef and chips and roast dinners (which were finished off with a fabulous ginger treacle pudding made by my Mum). This routine was hard to escape from when I finally left home at age eighteen. My Dad was fond of brains, tongue and tripe, which smelled horrible and made me feel sick. We also had funny names for things which my Dad made up, for example the small sharp kitchen knife, not to be used by youngsters, was called the 'cat stabber'. I think it was because Dad threatened to stab the pet cat, Fluffy, with the knife one time when it messed on the floor. The boys did try their hand at cooking, especially if they came home late for the evening meal. For these meals were always at set times. Once, Henry boiled a tin of baked beans in a saucepan of water without first making small holes in the lid, and it exploded all over the kitchen wall and cooker! What a mess of orange, nearly as bright as the other room's wallpaper!

I remember happy times when we used to celebrate fireworks night with a bonfire at the top of the drive, with jacket potatoes cooked in the fire. We never could afford many fireworks, but liked sparklers to wave around. Then we would watch our neighbour's fireworks from the windows. Caroline and I sometimes made a bonfire at the bottom of a friend's garden and fried sausages; they tasted so much better in the open air. Other happy and relaxing times were on Saturday mornings when we all listened to 'Round the Horne' and the children's radio programmes, such as 'Children's Hour' with Uncle Mac. My favourite songs were 'The Runaway Train', 'Sparky and the Magic Piano', 'Billy Goats Gruff', and 'The Laughing Policeman'. We drank orange squash while we listened (no fresh orange juice in those days, although we did have an orange vitamin drink from the Clinic when babies). Talking of drinks, I remember exactly when I had my first taste of the new Coca Cola! My brother Henry took Caroline and myself to a milk bar, called The Bread Basket, in London near where he was training to be a hairdresser. He quite casually said "I suppose you'll have a coke?" I had never heard of the lovely cool fizzy liquid but enjoyed it and have drunk it ever since.

My Parents

My Dad Joseph, known as Taffy, was born in South Wales into a large family in 1909. They lived at Dukestown near Tredegar in the Sirhowy valley. Dad had eight brothers and sisters and the family were poor. He was doing very well at school, but at fourteen he was forced to leave, as the family needed his wages. He worked in the Bedwelty coalmine in Ebbw Vale for six years, through the General Strike of 1926. He used to talk about the small donkeys used originally in the mines to pull trucks of coal, and about the use of birds in cages to indicate if there were poisonous gases around. His childhood contained tragedies, as two of his siblings died at an early age. One, Maria, burned to death when a fire started in the home. One sister, Lizzie, died in childbirth and two brothers, Henry and David died at the age of forty. (In later life two of his sisters, Jenny and Charlotte died of cancer.) When Joseph was twenty he could stand it no longer down the pit, and ran away to London to find a new future. He ended up sweeping up hair on a barber's floor and ultimately had his own barber's shop, first in Hoddesdon and then in Broxbourne in a little prefab which is still there today. He always spoke an Anglicised version of Welsh, wishing us goodnight (Nos da) and calling me darling (Cariad or Bach). He called our house the green gate in Welsh (llidiart gwyrdd) and that name stuck for a while. Most of his adult life he tried to learn one page a day of new words in the dictionary. He always impressed on me that learning and education meant you could get on in the world. As children he tested our spelling with spelling bees which always included the same words such as idiosyncrasy and antidisestablishmentarianism! I usually came top as I learnt the repeated words by heart.

Joseph was a convinced atheist and socialist. His hero was Aneurin Bevan, who laid the foundations for the Health Service in 1948. He often told me of the poor conditions of miners in South Wales, and he supported workers' rights and trade unions. No doubt he would have been staunchly behind the miners' cause in 1984 had he lived that long. (Sadly Dad died at the age of sixty-eight after lifelong abuse of his body with cigarettes and alcohol.)

My Mum May was from a small village family and was born in Debden near Saffron Walden in Essex in 1919. She had one sister, Jean, who was seven years her junior. The girls' Mum, Jessie, had epilepsy and was often shut away upstairs in the dark when she wasn't well. It wasn't known how to treat this condition at that time, and once the doctor painted my grandma from head to toe in iodine, which unsurprisingly made no difference. We were never allowed to venture upstairs in the cottage when my granny was resting. Mum always talked about her own school days, and her school reports show she was a quick learner and did well. She told me once that if she finished all her sums in good time she was asked to help out and sweep the school yard. She also helped younger children with their work. When May was seven one of her little friends, Lorna, died, and she often spoke of how upset she had been finding her friend collapsed in an outside toilet.

Mum's family lived in a thatched cottage, aptly named Rose Cottage because of the beautiful roses which grew near the door. My grandfather, also called Joseph, was a carpenter, but we did not know him for long. He grew vegetables in the garden, and I remember the gooseberries and the runner beans and fresh peas we used to pick. Beautiful sweet peas also grew there. At the back of the house in Debden was a field with a playground with an old swing which squeaked loudly, but no-one ever oiled the hinges. We also enjoyed the old rusty slide. There was an outside toilet (just a wooden lid and a pit) and a water barrel and the house had no electricity for years. My Great Aunt Bessie and Great Uncle Henry lived in the same village. Henry was a roof thatcher, and he had the habit of covering the settee with newspapers before he laid down for his afternoon rest; I suppose to keep it clean. Granny used to give us sweets out of a small glass jar with a stopper which she kept on the window ledge at Rose Cottage. That was our treat.

My Mum stayed at school till she was fifteen and then became a pupil teacher for a short while. Then she worked as a housemaid, in service to the big house Debden Manor. The area around there was lovely countryside, and years later when we visited, we spent a lot of time walking through the knee-high sweet-smelling cow parsley which bordered the meadows, down the lane to the old church. Mum's relatives were buried there amidst the overgrown grass. I liked to sit inside in the musty cool interior, where I could be alone to think. The village pond was always stagnant and covered with green slime, and to me looked dark and mysterious; what lurked beneath the surface? The lane was bordered by Horse Chestnut trees, and when in season we would collect the fallen conkers to play with at school.

My Dad used to spend hours in his favourite armchair, drinking Guinness and smoking. He usually had a stubbly chin and his fingers were yellow from the nicotine. He smoked all his life and never attempted to give up. Of course in those days the dangers of smoking were not fully realised. His nails were torn and broken, one or two missing. His hair was thick and ginger and later it turned grey. He wore a cravat, silky and green, around his neck, tucked into one of mum's home-knitted V neck sweaters, usually navy or dark green. He was short and quite plump. He wore baggy grey flannel trousers ordered cheap from the Daily Mirror advert, and he had suspenders to keep up his long socks. I can picture him now as though it were yesterday. I was close to my Dad and I think I saw a good side to him that my older siblings perhaps did not. If I was off school due to illness or, more usually tiredness (as I suffered from insomnia from an early age) I would sit opposite him on the other dark red tatty armchair while he stared, seemingly watching the stream of television programmes – the comedies, the documentaries, the sport (especially the snooker programmes such as Pot Black and the horse racing) and the all important news. Yet I grew to understand that his mind and his heart were not always there in that room. They wandered forlornly through his former life. He would reminisce about his childhood and his time down the pit, how he had fled to the big city, started a trade sweeping up on the barber's floor. Then, eventually, how he met my Mum, a gentle quiet village girl so lovely, innocent and shy. I think when he was a handsome young man he had fallen in love with Mum at the NAAFI where he was a cook, during the Second World War. He had a fondness for children and had five of his own over a period of ten years.

When he was drinking, Dad went through several stages. He would be at first lively and boisterous, then he would get angry and quite violent and afterwards he would fall into a long and depressive mood. Sometimes, though, the gentle joking man would slip through the morose exterior and it would be like old times. The stories told in a Welsh accent of the escapades of his youth. Yes, he had a great sense of humour and liked a good joke. (Sometimes he would go out to the outside toilet at Osborne Road and blow up the drainpipe of the adjacent bathroom while I was having a bath. At first I was taken by surprise but soon cottoned on to his prank. He could be heard laughing all the way back to the other room.) At the same time, he worried for his children. He wanted them to get a good education and to do well in life. He tried to prevent them from leaving home and venturing into a hostile world. He wanted them to stay in the nest, to stay close to him. For if the children got older then so must he, and loneliness turned him inside himself, bitter and afraid.

My Dad had his own rules in the house, and some were particularly strict. We had to ask to leave the table, were expected to help round the house, were not to use foul language and had to get to bed at a reasonable time. The girls were forbidden to wear make-up, nylons or any clothes which were too revealing. Dad often warned us of what would happen if we 'got in with boys' or 'opened our legs'. On the other hand he encouraged us to smoke and wanted us to sample alcohol. Two of my brothers ended up with a smoking habit but ultimately gave up years later. I smoked briefly as a student, more as a sociable habit, and soon gave up.

Dad was pretty unconventional and loved to get away without paying. Needless to say he was often the worse for wear when driving. He took us to the nearby gravel pits on a Sunday despite notices saying trespassers would be prosecuted and swimming was strictly forbidden. My brothers would swim there and, once, my Mum dropped her watch on the ground and it disappeared into the gravel, never to be found again even though we all searched. Dad would try to drive under the toll bar in the sewage works before the bar came down after the previous driver. This was a shortcut through the surrounding countryside and cost a shilling to pass through. Once the bar crashed down on the car and we only just made it through. Dad found it amusing.

He believed in 'keeping himself regular' with Beechams pills, and made sure we were each dosed with Senna Pods every weekend. This resulted in us all wanting the toilet desperately at the same time and made Sundays miserable times. What a character! (My Dad cut up newspaper pieces to be used in the toilet and my brother Stuart would spend what seemed like hours in there reading the fragments of stories on the newspaper!)

Believing in discipline and physical punishment, my Dad was quite Victorian in his attitudes. When fashions started to include the nylons introduced by Americans during the War, he would have none of it. I was condemned to wear three quarter woollen socks, albeit in bright colours. This caused humiliation at one school friend's party (aged eleven or twelve in 1963 or 64) when I was the ONLY girl wearing socks as everyone else had nylons! My sister Caroline was a very sociable girl, and as she was two years older than me she often met her friends in the evenings to go to the pictures or to stand at the bus stop and chat together. I found out early on that she went out wearing suitable clothes, but would change or adjust her skirt length and would apply make-up after leaving the house. On her return later in the evening she would remove her make up using Quickies moist pads, all so that Dad wouldn't lose his temper and call her names such as 'cheap tart'. If the worst happened and she was spotted, she'd be banned from going out for a while till she mended her ways and 'behaved like a lady'.

Dad kept his National Insurance Number on a tiny tatty piece of paper in his old wallet in his jacket just like I knew he would. He had it 'safe somewhere', he said. Dad asked me when I was about twelve to fill in his tax returns. He acquired an old typewriter and I used to do that job, as well as typing his bills for the tenants and any letters he sent. The information he gave me about his earnings was always a bit 'imaginative' to put it politely. His aim was to pay as little tax as possible; and his cash gained from running a few bets in the shop or for cutting and shaving a few extra customers was his business and no-one else's! This admin work set me on the road to writing. I wrote poems which I typed out, and at twelve began writing a diary which I have continued every day to the present.

Family Trips

When I was small, living at Broxbourne, we often had trips to Essex. On Sundays we would drive in the old Austin 7 into the country, usually to Debden village or to the weeping willow trees at Great Amwell by the New River. The car had wide running boards, a sliding roof and orange plastic indicators that came out of the side of the car as required. The route took us through a village called Ugly and that always made the children smile. One year that village won the most beautiful village prize, even with a name like that! The roof would be slid back on the car and one or two girls and boys would stand on the seat with our heads poked out, usually singing Dad's old favourite and familiar songs such as Danny Boy, Two Lovely Black Eyes, Johnnie's Lost His Marbles, Old Glasgow Town and of course the Welsh National Anthem. This last tune can always be guaranteed to bring tears to my eyes all these years later.

We used to stop at a crossroads in Essex, where there was a bluebell wood on the left and a pub on the right. Dad would get a beer, and we were treated to plain bags of Smiths Crisps with the small blue twists of salt inside. Sometimes I'd be lucky and get two packets of salt in one bag! When offered a choice of either Cherryade or Lemonade, Graham said he would have 'Anyade' and that name stuck for years. Mum loved to walk in the woods, but we didn't pick many bluebells as Mum said if everyone picked them there would be none left to enjoy. The flowers were beautiful, making a vivid blue carpet under the cool and shadowy trees.

Often we broke down or the car got overheated. Dad would 'tut tut' impatiently as he stuck his head under the bonnet. Once, Dad opened his car door suddenly and a passing car caught it and nearly knocked it off its hinges. Dad was furious.

One day when the sun was shining brightly we took the train to visit Springhall Road where my Great Aunt Bessie was living. My Auntie Jean, mum's sister, was visiting that day. My sister and I were dressed in matching royal blue cotton skirts with an illustration of lily of the valley flowers embroidered on the pockets. The day went well at first, but as usual I had an accident and had to turn my dress to the front and wear a cardigan around my waist to cover the wet patch. Caroline, who was more boisterous than me, ripped her skirt. We played in the garden until Mum said we could go for a walk to the local brook as long as we kept a close eye on little bother Graham, who was then about five years old.

We strolled down the lane to the stream, Caroline always laughing, teasing and taking charge. The field had many tree stumps on which wild mushrooms were growing. Cows and horses were running loose, and I felt scared of them. We went to pick pink Campion flowers which grew haphazardly on the bank of the stream. Graham was playing by the water and suddenly fell in. His short school trousers were soaked. I was at once very anxious; Mum would be cross. We made our way shamefacedly back to my Great Aunt's house, whereupon Mum was more upset than angry. How on earth could we go back on the train with Graham in dripping trousers? Reluctantly, a very embarrassed Mum asked for a loan from her sister, our Auntie Jean, and went to the local shop to buy a pair of shorts for Graham to wear for the journey home. Mum never had any ready cash as Dad only dolled it out in very small amounts. We all returned home rather subdued after what had promised to be a good day.

Years later when Great Auntie Bess was in a residential home in Bishops Stortford, Mum and I used to visit every Wednesday afternoon in the school holidays, while Dad had a half-day from work in the barber's shop. He would stay and cook liver for tea while we went on the train. Auntie Bess would be there waiting for us in a room near to her brother Uncle Henry's room. Uncle was not so well and we went to see him sleeping quietly under the covers of his bed. The rooms in the Home seemed tiny after Osborne Road. Auntie Bess thought of herself as upper class and believed in good manners. Her frequent saying was that you should not wear an apron to answer the door as this was common. We used to take Auntie Bessie humbugs to eat and she would give us Cadbury's chocolate miniatures in a blue box. She kept a stock of sweets for us, either in the wardrobe or in a cupboard which contained mothballs. As you can imagine they tasted really peculiar.

Childhood Memories

Although I had been told about a new baby, I did not really understand or appreciate what this would mean. I was three years old when the midwife brought in my little brother Graham, born at home in 1954, and laid him in the big red chair against the cushions. My two older brothers and my sister were at school, so I was privileged to get the first look at the new baby. The infant had tiny fragile fingers and toes, and he looked minute against the big armchair into which he was laid. (My earliest memory is of leaning backwards in this chair, sinking down and not being able to sit back up again.) My Auntie Jean smiled and carried Graham back to the bedroom where my Mum was recovering from the birth. Mum gave birth to all of her five children at home. That week when Graham was born my Dad was rushed to hospital with appendicitis, so Auntie Jean was in charge and she was very strict. She soon put paid to our antics such as jumping up and down on the beds! She even did some dusting, which my Mum never had the chance or energy to do.

As I have said I was a nervous child and felt uncomfortable in company. I used to blush painfully if spoken to, though in later years I did achieve some confidence when talking to people. I was a very quiet and shy girl, contrasting to my vociferous older sister. Now, many years later, I never stop talking, so it proves you can change if you want to! Added confidence makes a lot of difference.

My Infant and Junior School at Broxbourne was a lovely place. We walked along the leafy banks of the New River canal, glimpsing the blue flash of the kingfishers on the banks and fish in the water. It was a small school, and though I was nervous at first I came to enjoy the work which I found easy. We used to have a regular 'nature table', and I loved finding specimens to display; acorns, conkers, birds' eggs, feathers, fir cones and autumn leaves. In charge were the two Miss Coxes (sisters) who were firm but fair. The only bad incident which I remember was when a girl called Esther had her hair pulled by the teacher when she was no good at mental arithmetic. This made her cry. Generally, reading was encouraged, but by then I loved it already. One of my favourite teachers, Mr. Bassett, introduced us to the Borrower stories by Mary Norton, and I took part in the nationwide Cadbury's competition about the production of coal and its side products such as soap. I got highly commended for that. In the play ground, my friends and I used to play endless clapping rhymes and skipping games which required singing and holding hands like 'In and Out the Dusty Bluebells'.

When I was nine (in September 1960) we were allowed out during lesson time one day to witness the total eclipse of the sun. This was quite scary, when everything went dark and still. Shortly afterwards the birds flew frantically back to the trees. I have never forgotten it.

From an early age I loved reading. Every Saturday morning I would go to the local library at Hoddesdon, firstly accompanied by Mum or an older brother and then on my own or with Graham. The library was housed in an old house and museum at that time. One Saturday when three year old Graham was kept quiet with a small white paper bag of sweets (lemonade powder I think), he caused amusement in the library when he said in a loud voice: 'This bag is dilapidated!' I loved Milly-Molly-Mandy books, and likened in my mind the adventures Graham and I took, exploring our surroundings to Milly's adventures in the woods or by the river all day with only a slice of white bread and butter to sustain her. I also enjoyed "Wind in the Willows" and the beautiful descriptions of the riverside. I progressed to "Swallows and Amazons", Biggles books and other adventure stories. I read every book in sight and at the age of eight or nine asked if I could use the adult library, and I was allowed to. After that I read every classic novel that I came across. Watching the assistants and the librarian working in that peaceful, calm and quiet and (to me) wonderful environment meant a lot, and I decided very early on that that's what I wanted to do when I grew up. At Grammar School I became a Library helper, which was my first step towards becoming a Librarian many years later.

At home we didn't have many books, but my Dad did give us a collection of encyclopaedias one Christmas as he always regretted the interruption to his own education. All of us had an Annual every Christmas; mine was Bunty or Judy. The comics of the same names often gave free gifts of bracelets or necklaces made of plastic poppers, and I was thrilled to receive them. My older brothers liked Beano or Dandy, Andy Capp or Giles, and Graham had Rupert annuals. Outside in the garden we played for hours, not with today's plastic toys, but we improvised with old cereal packets, pieces of grass, horse chestnuts and acorns. I used to have imaginary tea parties using lemonade as tea and sorrel as sugar, with my dolls on a blanket on the lawn; years later I would lie there listening to pirate radio stations, flicking through magazines. The gravel drive and flat areas in the garden were used to mark out dinky car tracks, with pretend garages and bridges. As children we tried communicating using two treacle tins (green and gold golden syrup tins) and a length of string. Amazingly it worked quite well! As a family we played a lot of games, including card games such as 'Beat Your Neighbour Out Of Doors' and our own devised version of 'Cheat', which caused giggling and hilarity. Henry used to construct amazing items out of metal Meccano; this being the pre-Lego era. Stuart and later Graham constructed Airfix aeroplanes. Monopoly and Scrabble were also popular, but caused many arguments over who was cheating or inventing words.

Cheat is a simple card game for three or more players. First deal the cards evenly between the players. Player one puts any Aces they may hold face down in the middle of the table, stating aloud the cards they've discarded, for example, "Two Aces". Players then take it in turns to remove cards from their hand in the same way, following the sequence Ace to King, returning to Ace etc. The player first to get rid of all their cards wins – simple! The catch is, as the name suggests, you don't have to honestly describe the cards you've discarded. Players can challenge each other by saying "Cheat!" at any time; and play stops to check the cards on top of the discarded pile. If the accusation proves to be true, the 'cheat' has to pick up all the cards from the middle of the table, but if the accusation is unfounded the accuser has to pick up all the cards instead. We had endless fun with this game.

I remember a toy shop in Hoddesdon High Street which held a fascination for us. It was a narrow shop which reached a long way back, and as you progressed further into the shop the toys seemed to become more intriguing and special. We never had much money to spend on toys, only if we had saved birthday money or pocket money, but it was so exciting and enjoyable to look.

My sister Caroline was already at school when I started attending, and once or twice she had to come and find me and take care of me when I was upset about something. My youngest brother didn't settle into school when he was five. In fact he climbed a tree in our garden and refused to come down, as he wanted to stay at home with Mum. In later years he was bullied at school so I tried to keep an eye out for him.

For a very short time Caroline and I attended Sunday school at the scout hut on the edge of the recreation ground. My Dad, who was not a believer, gave us the choice whether to continue attending or not; we both declined happily and found other things to do with our time.

We used to do country dancing at our Junior School, and used a Maypole. The idea was that you clutched a piece of coloured ribbon attached to the pole and danced in a circle while going over one child's ribbon and under another, creating a sort of coloured plait. I wasn't very good at this and messed things up when I got the coloured ribbons tangled when I danced the wrong way. For the weekly lessons of country dancing in the school hall, the boys had to first choose a partner. I always got chosen by Stephen who was heavily built and inevitably trod on my toes while dancing. He was a boastful arrogant boy and I didn't like him.

I encountered awkward situations socially. I once went to a birthday party at Stephen's house in a nearby road called Churchfields, and I had never had tinned salmon before (a luxury we couldn't afford!) and I didn't know what it was. I had to watch my manners and tried not to show that I was of a lower social order. One friend had some glove puppets, and we performed little shows from behind thick velvet curtains in her 'posh' house. Another friend had two small poodles, both white, and I started to yearn for a pet dog of my own. Other friends' houses were neat, clean, tidy and well decorated, and I soon realised we weren't quite as well to do as fellow pupils.

Barber's shop

As I have said, my Dad had his own barber's shop with the red and white striped pole outside. The building was a prefab. It was quite small, but was divided into a ladies' stylists one side and a gents' barbers the other side. He used old but sharp cut throat razors on the gentlemen customers. When I was ten or eleven I started helping out at the shop, which meant dusting the glass shelves which contained bottles of Silvikrin shampoo and Vitalis and Brylcreem hair lotion for men, and sweeping up the hair from the floor into a small cubby-hole. From there, Dad scooped it up into the dust bin. Also, I used to tidy up the drawers where Dad kept betting slips, cheques and receipts. He took bets on the horses from the shop. On one occasion I was very puzzled to find packets of condoms in the drawer, as I had NO idea what they were for. I think after unfolding one of them I did sort of understand it! My Dad used to always ask his male customers if they needed 'something for the weekend' and I presumed it was chocolates to give to their wives. Oh, the innocence of youth!

Often we called into Dad's shop on our way back from school, and he would let us have packets of Rowntree's fruit gums or fruit pastilles to eat. The shop had a cigarette machine outside and also sold Wrigley's chewing gum. Dad would take a break morning and afternoon, and boil some milk up on his small gas ring to make the milky coffee which he loved. The shop was near the recreation ground where we often took a walk. There was a spinney, and a slide and swings nearby. One afternoon after school when I was dawdling through the trees I was approached by a scruffy man who exposed himself to me. I showed bravado and said

I had seen it all before as I had three brothers and that my Dad was nearby in the shop and he would come and get the man. I never told anyone about that episode, even though I thought it hadn't upset or frightened me. The man was reported at school and the Head Mistress warned us to keep away from the spinney but I kept quiet.

Dad never made much money from his haircuts or taking bets. When I was ten I went on a holiday to Swanage in Dorset with the school. It was the first time I had been away from home, and an experience I didn't wholly enjoy because I was so travel sick. I was also desperately homesick. When it came to paying for the trip most pupils paid all at once, but Dad gave me a ten shilling note from the shop till every week till it was paid off. This was rather humiliating for me as everyone got to know that I had to pay in instalments! Whilst away I found I couldn't sleep, and was disappointed when there were only a couple of letters from home. I was not used to being away on my own.

Leisure Time

In the summer months during those days of sunny childhood never forgotten, we would go swimming at the open air pool at nearby Hoddesdon. It was an outdoor pool, so quite cold in the cooler months of the year. In fact, we used to go there with the school too, and the crocodile of children would walk right past our house on their way to swimming lessons. When Dad came with the family to the pool he proved he was a confident swimmer, but when I was quite small he threw me in the cold water in an effort to force me to learn to swim! I was very shocked, cold and shivering and extremely scared. However, I did manage to waggle my arms and legs and get to the pool side so I suppose his method worked! My Dad looked older than anyone else's (he was ten years older than my Mum) and his chest sprouted white hairs. His chin was usually unshaven too, and my loyalty for my Dad was torn by embarrassment in front of my friends. Some teased me that he looked more like a grandad!

My Dad didn't like holidays. In fact, I only remember him going away when he visited relatives in South Wales. Once he did drive us to North Wales, where he had booked accommodation, deliberately omitting to mention that he was bringing his FIVE children with him! (He was hoping to save money!) The landlady was amazed when we all piled out of the car, and of course had to turn us away. From there we went to stay at Butlins at Pthwelli which cost more than we had planned. However, we enjoyed the amusements and the food; porridge being my favourite meal of the day. Another holiday was in a cottage somewhere in North Wales, which had an organ on which we endlessly played the tune, 'Oh Will You Wash My

Father's Shirt'. The house had an intriguing corridor which circled from back to front.

When I was thirteen we went on a holiday without Dad to Cornwall, and stayed in a caravan at Newquay. My eldest brother Henry took his girlfriend, plus her brother and girlfriend. Various complicated sleeping arrangements were made, with the young people sleeping at a nearby bed and breakfast. The beaches were out of this world, wide stretches of unbroken sand, rock pools and even caves. I suppose it was the first proper holiday that we had as a family, even though Dad wasn't there. (Previously, apart from the abortive trips to Wales, we had only managed day trips on the train to Southend or Clacton). The sun shone and we paddled in the sea, explored the caves and befriended a couple of donkeys in the nearby field. Each day we would be treated to a cornet full of yellow Cornish ice cream. Those were happy times. On the way back home we even stopped to take a look at Stonehenge; in those days you could walk right up and touch the monument.

My brother Henry bought a rowing boat which had an outboard motor. This boat (called 'Jada' after a pop song, then 'Twister' when the twist came into fashion) was berthed on the nearby River Lea and sometimes Henry would take us out one at a time for a row. I found I was good at rowing, but Mum was always scared of the water. That was when I learned to row with my strong arms along the green bordered banks and lovely scenery of Broxbourne and Dobbs Weir. (I remember that one time Henry fell into the rushing water of the weir but managed to swim to safety; and another occasion when my youngest brother Graham jumped up on the bank of the New River and fell in. One of us pulled him out and he was none the worse for his little trip.) Graham and I were both fascinated by water and often went down to the rivers to play. We were once caught throwing stones (trying to skim them) into the canal, the New River, and an eager policeman cautioned us and said it was illegal to do that as this was drinking water for the surrounding area. Many family walks took place by these two rivers as the scenery was very pleasant, and we often saw the brightly coloured kingfishers flash by.

The River Lea was bordered by rows of quite big and expensive houses. Some had their own boats moored up, and there was a wooden-fronted rowing club on the further bank. In Junior School I had a friend called Deborah who was lucky to live in one of those houses, and I loved to play in her garden. Sometimes we would swim in the river, but it wasn't really allowed. We used to play imaginative games involving fairy stories and wild adventures around those river banks, and were away from home for hours on end. Those were not the days of mobile phones and our house never even had a telephone till much later than other neighbours. A ten minute walk to the call box often became a necessity, using old two pence coins and the button A and B system. Mum didn't worry about us being out as long as we were home by dark.

We hardly ever locked our door in those days! The house had a huge heavy mortise key which, if we were going out to the shops or a walk, we would leave in the gutter above the small shed next to the outside toilet. At some point that shed became Graham's and he would build wooden models and such for many hours. Previously pet rabbits and a hedgehog were kept in the shed, but were let loose on the grass every day.

Under The Magnolia Trees

A young friend once showed me her stick insects kept in a large glass sweetie jar in her bedroom. I didn't like crawly things, but these two just kept still most of the time and were camouflaged with the twigs in the jar. I did enjoy watching them, hoping they would move, but they rarely did. When my friend went on holiday for a week I was given the jar and full charge of the stick insects. I kept them in the outside shed and put their food in every day. One day I must have carelessly left the lid off, only to find the two insects had crawled away. I felt very guilty and enrolled my siblings to search for them but we never found them. When my friend arrived back from her break I had to confess and she was very upset and hardly spoke to me again. At least, I thought, the stick insects had gained their freedom and were no longer confined to a glass jar.

I used to nag and pester my parents at length if I wanted something. When I was twelve and thirteen I became obsessed with getting a puppy of my own after reading a book called 'A Dog So Small' by Phillippa Pearce. The boy in the story wanted a dog so badly that he came to believe in a small imaginary Chihuahua dog which went with him everywhere. Finally after some hysterics on my part we went up to London's Petticoat Market one Sunday morning by train and collected a small mongrel pup which I christened Bozo after a little dog Caroline used to draw sometimes. In hindsight, the poor dog was taken from its mother too early and we never trained him. As he had some Alsatian in him he was a bit wild and out of control. We used to let him run free in the garden and often he would roam the area. Bozo got very agitated and excited when we came home or if we had a visitor at the door, but I was devoted to him and cared for him as best as I knew how. After a year or two, the obvious thing happened when Bozo chased and bit a young girl in our road and it was decided that he would have to be put down. It wasn't the dog's fault, and I didn't realise how he should have been trained and kept on a lead. I was heartbroken when the dog was put down by the PDSA (we couldn't afford a vet's fees) and became quite miserable over the whole thing. I had loved him dearly.

As children I think we all learned to ride a bicycle, and they were handed down to each child as they grew to fit the size. (Also I had a phase of trying to roller skate, but I wasn't very good and skinned my knees regularly.) Once, when Henry had the wheels of his bicycle revolving in front of him on the back step, he hurt his finger when it got caught in the spokes. He came running in with blood dripping from his hand and had to go to hospital. My younger brother Graham and I spent many long and happy hours cycling round the area. One of our games was doing figures of eight on the road, for there was hardly any traffic there in the fifties. On other days we went to the local Broxbourne woods, where we picked blackberries or sloes. My Dad had a friend called Percy who would occasionally bring us a rabbit for tea from the woods. At the River Lea or the New River canal, we tried to catch small fish with our fishing nets, but we were never very good at it and only threw the fish back into the water when we did catch them. We traced the course of Spital brook which flowed alongside our road (in our wellies) sometimes damming it for fun, and spent many hours exploring the neighbourhood fields and pathways. Graham was three years younger than me and I could boss him about a bit as my sister did to me. Actually when I went to school I befriended children younger than me, perhaps because I could handle them better and didn't like being dominated by a more confident child.

Jobs and Hobbies

My first job was the sweeping up of hair on the barber's floor (my Dad's shop), but shortly after that Graham and I were employed to walk a dog owned by some friends of Stuart's, the Smiths. Mr. and Mrs Smith lived in a posh house up near Broxbourne Woods, and their dog was a big Alsatian. I think he was called Bengy. I was certainly a bit scared of Bengy, but during our walks amongst the trees, usually after school, the dog was always well behaved. This particular way of earning more pocket money was curtailed a couple of years later when Bengy turned aggressively against the son of the family, Roderick, and bit his arm. Following that job, Graham and I had a short-lived leaflet delivery round. It became extremely boring to do, and the walking up and down the long drives, which many of the houses had, soon got tedious. At first we would try to take short cuts across one garden to the next to cut corners, but were swiftly told off by the residents who didn't want their lawns and flower beds damaged. Then we tried to discreetly drop wadges of leaflets in the bins, pretending we had delivered them all. We soon got found out and that was the end of that small earner! I then worked in a local baker's shop in the Broxbourne parade on a Saturday; a job which was originally Caroline's and which made me popular with my siblings because the left over cream cakes could be taken home and eaten!

The summer before University at the age of eighteen, I worked on a till in the Sainsbury's at Hoddesdon, which was a hard job, consisting of long days (nine a.m. till eight p.m.) and which in those days had certain pitfalls. If your till didn't balance at the end of the shift and it was more than two and sixpence out then you had to make up the discrepancy. Once my till was five pounds out and I had to pay that back out of a wage which was only small. How easy it was to give a note too much back as change when you were flustered. However, I made friends with an older lady called Jean, who used to make me giggle. We both got a bit hysterical at the end of a working day. When I had to redo a whole bill because I had made one error (punching in the items and the amounts individually in a time before scanners), Jean would save the day with her sense of humour, calling out the items and amounts till we got to the end of the customer's bill.

I had various hobbies to keep myself occupied. I used to collect recipes and copy them out with three coloured biros into a folder which was intended to eventually become a complete Cookbook of my own devising. I never did get it finished! Also I liked to sew and to knit: at first clothes for my doll Maggie, then jumpers for the family. At the age of fourteen (in 1965) I started making a quilt from knitted hexagon shapes of all different colours; I eventually finished that in time for my son's birth in 1980. I kept a daily diary from the age of twelve and devoured books. Sometimes I collected wild flowers, which I identified from my Ladybird Book on flowers and pressed under the carpet, displaying them in a scrapbook. I had a phase of collecting doll's furniture, but some was too expensive for my pocket. We always had pocket money, but had to earn it by doing chores, and it didn't go far.

Being a Girl/ Grammar School Days

I was never told the facts of life as a girl. When I went to secondary school we were given a talk about sanitary towels and not putting them down the toilets. I had no clue of what was being talked about but didn't let on. A few days later a fellow pupil dropped a tampon (very new at that time, 1962) on the floor and I said to her 'What's that for?' Nervously she explained, and I felt such a fool. When my own periods started I was alarmed, and although I had promised Caroline to go swimming that day, I said I couldn't go after all. After explaining to Mum (who was painfully embarrassed when dealing with such matters) she told Caroline why I couldn't go to the pool. Mum also told my Dad who made some remark about me 'now being a woman'. I was twelve or thirteen and certainly didn't feel like a woman!

My Grammar School in Ware (later renamed 'Presdales School for Girls') was very upper class. I had passed my eleven plus with ease and went to the new school in 1962. I felt out of my depth all the time I was there (seven years). I was pulled up on my accent and my best friend used to coach me in things like pronouncing 'restaurant' with a weak 't'. This same friend, Lesley, came from an upper class family, whilst mine was definitely working class. I suppose I only progressed upwards in the social ranks when I obtained a place at university – only the top 5 % of the population did so at that time. Lesley used to take me to the theatre, ballet and opera, and talked to me about politics and books; she individually helped to 'improve me'!! She introduced me early on to the Greek singer Nana Mouskouri, and we went to many of her concerts in London.

When we had 'tea' in our house it was at 5.30pm and consisted of egg and chips or stew with the family on a very casual basis. Lesley's Mum used to serve 'dinner' at 7.30pm with napkins and wine, and it was what I called a 'posh' meal, like beef bourguignon. I had once failed a test at Brownies because I did not lay the table properly. Well, I had never seen fish knives or steak knives and had never heard of a 'cruet'! The Brown Owl took pity on me and gave me a quick lesson in the order of how to lay knives, forks and spoons on the table, and different courses of a meal. In the end I passed and got my badge but it was a bit of a humiliating experience! I left the Brownies under a bit of a cloud at age seven or eight when I laughed so much that I wet the floor! If I remember rightly Caroline and I got the giggles.

The girls at the Grammar School lived in posh houses in well-to-do areas. Our motley family let the side down really, though we were happily oblivious to this when children. One or two neighbours (such as Mrs. Hobhouse from around the block) thought we lowered the tone of the area and that the kids 'ran wild' in our family. My Dad would get cross when hearing that and said we had every right to live there – as much as anyone else. The girls at school had exotic names such as 'Suella', 'Theodora' and 'Valetta', and took holidays abroad; their families often went skiing abroad or owned a yacht, which was not too common at this time. I struggled to hold my head up amongst them, and my Mum was completely out of her depth at school functions. She used to get very nervous at school events and once didn't realise you had to stand up for the Nation Anthem (which I found humiliating). My Dad never ever attended Parents' evenings or school events. I only had gym slips handed down from Caroline; we could not afford new ones, and I was embarrassed by the state of my clothes. My hair was usually a mess, often tangled after a sleepless night, so you could not get a comb through it. I was permanently anxious during lessons. However I did make good friends while at school, some of whom I kept in touch with through later life.

For many years I was jealous of my sister, but later I realised we had a lot in common; both married with a child or two, and occasionally finding things hard. Caroline was very popular and seemed full of self confidence, and had many friends. I found it hard to maintain friendships until I was older, and I often trailed behind her and her pals, getting on her nerves. At Grammar School the teachers used to call me 'Caroline's sister', and it took ages and lots of hard work to establish myself in my own right. Caroline was Head Girl at Presdales all girls' School, and she was a heroine (much admired by me) when she managed to get the compulsory wearing of the school beret abolished before she left for Teacher Training College in Cheshire at the age of eighteen.

The Grammar School was seven miles away from Broxbourne, and every day we travelled on the bus (which made me feel sick) to Ware. There we had to climb a steep hill, which never got any easier over the years. The school at the top of the road was based in an old house with modern extensions built onto it. The journey used to make me tired, but chatting to friends was a pleasant way to pass the time. I grew in confidence as I made good friends such as Myra and Lesley. My girl friends envied me my three brothers and liked to hear about them, and they 'fancied' Stuart in particular. Stuart went to the local boys' Grammar School in Hertford, and thus could sometimes be spotted on the upstairs deck of the local bus. I also used to notice an older boy who got on and off at our bus stop, but I never ever plucked up the courage to speak to him. As Presdales was single sex, all the girls went haywire in their excitement if a man was seen on the premises. The only two male teachers we had were both dismissed for inappropriately touching pupils, one in the science labs and the other in Latin lessons after lunchtime in the pub. The latter, Mr Jones, was always drunk after lunch and used to ask me and other girls to sit alongside him in front of the class while he marked our homework. His arm would sneak across my shoulder and down the front of my body, while he told the rest of the class to get on with the set work. His breath used to be foul but I didn't dare push him away.

I particularly enjoyed learning French because I liked the teacher Miss Hodge, who seemed ancient to us but was probably only in her forties. Miss Hodge had white hair and used to relate a story of how her hair became white. Apparently she was engaged during the Second World War to a young man she adored. When he was killed in action her hair turned white overnight and had stayed the same ever since.

In 1963 there was a very bad winter with heavy and prolonged snowfalls. The school made an exception to the uniform rules and allowed girls to wear trousers to school for the first time ever. I still remember trudging for weeks through the blizzards, slushy snow and ice to reach school. In later years part of Ware College at the foot of the big hill got used for school lessons, and it was a relief not to have to make that climb.

On one or two occasions, my friend Lesley and I presented the morning assembly at school. First it was on the theme of apartheid, and we read from 'Cry the

Beloved Country' by Alan Paton and played a song by Paul Robeson. Another time we read pieces from the newspaper on the topic of the Arab/Israeli Six Day War of 1967. I think I became more politically aware because of Lesley's influence. I enjoyed writing at school, particularly poems and composition. Once I was asked to read my poem about the sea to the whole class because it had been the best that month:

The Sea

The feeling of sand underfoot,

Soft and warm.

Trickles of water

Down a cliff face,

Like a mountain

It seemed to me.

Cool ice-cream, pretty shells,

And the water... the water,

Stretching on forever

And out of sight...

And the <u>feel</u> of the water splashing at my ankles,

And the smells in the breeze:

Of sea, of salt... of happiness.

And the girl on the donkey,

Nodding its dark head

At the flies.

And the water... the water,

Under The Magnolia Trees

The SEA.

Ware Grammar School
January 1965 (aged 13)

Another poem which featured in my life at that time was "We are the Music Makers" by Arthur O'Shaughnessy. I can only recall the first verse:

"We are the music makers
And we are the dreamers of dreams
Standing by lone sea breakers
And sitting by desolate streams
World losers and world forsaken
On whom the pale moon gleams
But we are the movers and the shakers
Of the world forever, it seems…"

Lesley taught me this poem and said it had inspired her to think that she could achieve anything she wanted in her life. (She proved over the years that it was true, overcoming serious illness, having children against the odds and following a career in the legal profession in another country.)

We were allowed to listen to records in the school hall at lunch times and could watch tennis matches from Wimbledon after our exams were finished. In fact I was quite good at tennis, though short in stature, and spent many lunchtimes at Presdales playing in a foursome. I even had some coaching at the Broxbourne Lawn Tennis Club (a very posh venue) but it was too expensive for me to continue. After years of listening to the pirate Radio Caroline, the Radio One music channel was launched and in 1963 the Beatles music swept through the country and we loved it. The girls in my class endlessly discussed which records were our favourites and which Beatle we preferred. Most girls loved Paul but I secretly admired John. We swapped photos of 'the fab four' torn from girlie magazines. We used to dance with each other and try to do the twist and the locomotion. One girl was suspended when found drinking whisky at one of these lunchtime 'parties'. Another girl was expelled for becoming pregnant – I don't know how she managed that as I never met any boys except my own brothers.

Lesley, my tall slim best friend developed cancer (Hodgkin's disease) when we were at school at the age of seventeen. She was in hospital for some months and I missed her badly. I took it on myself to copy up each lesson for her and to send notes with a fellow pupil on the school bus to Lesley's home so she could keep up with the work as far as possible. I also took on her Editorship of the School Magazine that year and found I was capable of doing it and enjoyed the writing and editing very much. Eventually, Lesley got better and came back to school. As far as I know she has kept reasonably well ever since. She was/is the sort of person who can achieve anything, who overcame obstacles, and I admired her and learned a lot from her friendship.

Nervous Times for Mum and Me

My mum was a nervous creature who constantly worried about small things (where did I get it from?). She struggled to get through the daily grind of washing, cooking and housework and caring for five lively children, very close in age. Her household budget was minimal, and each extra item she requested such as a pair of nylons for herself resulted in my Dad counting out the exact cost (or what he mistakenly underestimated as the cost) into her palm. She often had to wait for ages to get new things, and rarely had any new clothes or personal things for herself. All the money went on food or school lunch money or whatever was needed that week.

My hard-working mum had straight brown hair which she clipped back from her face. She wore pinafore dresses in dull colours, or trousers with jumpers for comfort. She never wore make-up, and her complexion stayed smooth and young looking for many years. She rarely wore jewellery or had occasion to dress up. She was the kindest of people but was often anxious, especially if she felt out of her social class, such as when mixing with school teachers or posh parents. Mum tried her best always and tried to keep the peace within the family unit despite the upsets caused by Dad's drinking and subsequent bad temper.

I was a nervous and sensitive child who often remained silent when the family rows were going on. I used to have emotional tantrums and was often crying over something or other. Sometimes I would literally bang my head against the wall for several minutes until I was taken notice of. Because I was often miserable, I lived up to my nickname 'Moaning Minnie'. I was timid at school, though bright. The main family problems were caused by lack of money and by my Dad's drinking. When I look back now, I believe he was an alcoholic, but nothing was ever said about that at the time. Arguments would take place between my Dad and my two older brothers, and Dad often shouted at Mum or at the younger children. When he wasn't at his barber's shop a short distance away, he drank heavily at home, usually Guinness. He was known to threaten us with his leather belt, but rarely caught us as we were too nimble. Once or twice my older brothers would step into a row to separate my parents and to stop Dad hitting Mum. My Mum was of a nervous disposition, but was strong in her own way, as she managed to cope with years and years of these sorts of atmospheres. I suffered agonies of anxiety when arguments broke out, and this I think was the start of my nervous problems.

Although the girls, Caroline and I, helped as much as we could, there was hardly a moment in the day when Mum wasn't working. She used to do the ironing in the evenings after tea while we settled down to watch television (we only got one of these in about 1960). We used to enjoy the first episodes of Coronation Street, and the newly emerging programmes about pop music: Ready Steady Go, 6-5 Special, Juke Box Jury and eventually Top of the Pops. While we sipped orange squash and ate a packet of Smiths crisps and relaxed, Mum would be sweating away with the iron. Often Dad would be eating his tea of tripe and onions or fried cheese done in the bottom of a frying pan. He worked of course, but was usually sedentary while at home, and he took for granted that Mum would keep daily chores up to date. Mum often got very weary, and when I was twelve, she had to go into hospital for a hysterectomy operation. She lost a lot of weight and was told to rest when she came home; what a joke, she didn't have a chance of that. Caroline and I helped out as much as we could, taking over her jobs while she was in her sick bed, but she took a while to recover her strength.

As a family, we had our usual illnesses and accidents. Both of my parents were troubled with stomach ulcers, and Dad had to go into hospital at one point when he was in a lot of pain. Mum used to play down her suffering then, as she often did when she had a headache. Dad had his appendix removed and later in life had several strokes, became diabetic and developed gangrene in both legs. Caroline used to suffer from migraines, probably due to the day-to-day stresses in the household. Stuart had an accident in which he fractured his pelvis, and we visited him in hospital while he recovered. Henry once turned his car over near Broxbourne Parade and it rolled off the grassy bank, but he seemed to emerge quite unscathed. I never broke any limbs; it was always my mind which was unsettled.

Mum was very loyal to her family and did her best to care for us all. Not an easy task, with the shortage of money and with my Dad's drunken bouts most weeks. Dad would get into arguments with her or the children and used to shout and get very angry. I was sensitive to these outbursts, and they would make me very miserable and anxious. I thought this sort of carry on was 'normal' for families, until I eventually talked to school friends and discovered that this was far from true.

I had my homework to complete every night, and we seemed to get a lot of it at Grammar School. I got extremely stressed due to the pressure of the quantity of homework and the exams; it affected my sleeping and my nerves were often on edge. My parents were unable to help with homework as they did not have much of an education. I got snappy and irritable and often made an emotional scene which would irritate my sister particularly. Eventually I would calm down, but I often failed to relax.

During revision for O levels and A levels I got extremely stressed, although perversely I got good grades. I was taken to the doctor several times, but I refused to take the tranquilisers which were offered, around the age of fifteen. I was worried they would prove to be addictive and would badly affect my brain long term. Perhaps if I had taken the medication then, which would have helped the chemical imbalance in my brain, I would not have experienced the four breakdowns which followed in my adult life. I think I was suffering from depression from the age of about fifteen, but I knew little about the condition and my parents were at a loss to help me. This was all to build up to my first psychotic breakdown in 1971 when I was twenty. By then I had gone to University (in Sheffield), the first ever in my family to do so, and struggled to cope away from home. I didn't make friends at first, and found it so hard even to walk into a room of unknown students. I missed my family and its routines but could seldom afford to travel home for a visit. My mum wrote regularly, and this correspondence was a lifesaver to me. Ultimately I did find like-minded friends and started to socialise, but 'cracked up' in my second year at University, an episode which had been building up I think for a long, long time. This period of my life I have written about in more detail in my book "The Nest of Sanity".

There are many factors which contributed to my emotional problems, including of course genetic traits. I did struggle as a child and I still do today, but am far more content. I can see the roots of my mental health problems in my childhood experiences. I was unsettled by the arguments in the household, and indeed the verbal if not physical violence between my older brothers and my Dad and between Mum and Dad. I was constantly anxious and slept badly. My Mum's stress rubbed off on me. This did not mean I was not fond of and close to my Dad. I tried to understand his behaviour and always forgave him after his outbursts. I had plenty of my own fluctuations of mood and caused problems in the family myself. I used to be jealous of my sister and argued with her a lot, often physically scratching and tussling with her.

Another symptom of my anxiety was wetting the bed, which I did until I was about nine years old. I even wet myself at school a few times, and humiliatingly one time it was at Brownies at the age of seven and I never again returned there, due to the embarrassment. A big factor was insomnia, which I still suffer from. Without restful sleep I was often on edge, and had quite a few days off school because I hadn't slept well, and Mum would take pity on me and let me catch up with sleep during the day. My mind gets so active and goes over and over problems and plans for hours. I have always wished I could have an OFF switch for my brain! This problem didn't improve when I left home, but I now have certain methods of relieving my insomnia which includes more exercise, long relaxing baths and sometimes taking a sleeping pill.

In my adult life, as I said, I have suffered four nervous breakdowns and periods of severe depression. These were described in my book 'The Nest of Sanity'. Now in my late fifties, partly due to medication, I feel and cope much better, although I do have difficult times. I am calmer, and am able to look back and reflect on my childhood days without resentment or regret.

Finally

There were happy times in my childhood, as I have described. My siblings were and are an excellent bunch of people and my parents did their best in the most difficult circumstances. I do not hold anything against my Dad or my Mum for being the people they were. How I wish I could have them back in my life, so I could say all those things I never said when they were alive. Many happy occasions still remain in my memories. Above all, I remember the big house at Osborne Road, shown on the cover of this book, and those magnificent flowering magnolia trees which I will never forget...